Folding the Real

for Swithin

FIONA SAMPSON

Folding the Real

[signature]
21·VII·03

seren

seren
is the book imprint of
Poetry Wales Press Ltd
Nolton Street, Bridgend, Wales
www.seren-books.com

© Fiona Sampson, 2001

The right of Fiona Sampson to be identified as the
Author of this Work has been asserted in
accordance with the Copyright, Designs and
Patents Act, 1988.

ISBN 1-85411-297-X

A CIP record for this title is available from
the British Library

All rights reserved. No part of this publication
may be reproduced, stored in a retrieval system,
or transmitted at any time or by any means
electronic, mechanical, photocopying, recording
or otherwise without the prior permission
of the copyright holders.

*The publisher works with the financial assistance of the
Arts Council of Wales*

Cover Photograph by Iosif Kiraly

Printed in Palatino by
Bell & Bain Ltd, Glasgow

Contents

- 7   But Summer Light
- 8   The Honeymooneers
- 9   From the Scots
- 10   Into the Dark
- 11   Wulf and Eadwacer
- 12   How It Was
- 13   Logging the Windfall
- 15   Putting the Field Together
- 16   The Separation
- 19   Walking, Flying
- 20   The Hand, Dreaming
- 21   Landscapes After Verlaine
- 21   I. Shepherd's Delight
- 22   II. Autumn Number
- 23   III. Deep Water
- 24   Cut Glass
- 25   Hotel Boulevard
- 27   Hors d'Oeuvre
- 28   Tracking
- 29   Getting the Results
- 30   The X File
- 31   The Misunderstanding
- 32   Drawing the Line
- 33   A Family Affair
- 33   I. Born 1899: A Costive Incubation
- 34   II. Born 1932: The Eggshell Cadenza
- 35   III. Born 1963: Flying the Nest
- 36   The Bargain
- 37   Draft for a Short Fiction
- 38   Fear of Drowning
- 39   Folding the Real
- 40   Dear Emma

42	What Furniture Does
43	Pastoral from a Millennial Pattern-Book
44	Wye
45	Travel Diary
46	Metamorphosis
47	Viznar by Moonlight: Two poems after Lorca
47	I. The Moon's Up
48	II. The Night of Loving Sleeplessly
49	Sestina for an Ice Age
51	The Pull of Air
52	Icarus in a Rainstorm (Six Views)
54	Legal and Tender
55	The Science of Memory
56	The Fattening
57	Green Thought I-V
63	By Your Self
64	*Acknowledgements*

But Summer Light

But summer light, which starts out as modulations of smoke
among trees, and which gathers types of pallor to itself
like a gothic hagiography, making content form,
confusing the eye with something splendidly implied, must move
      which it does, hammering after-all-exact facets
to each wall, dormer, chimney bracket and pipe of the now-
illuminated town so that like a calendar it
presents the eye with complexity, the severalness
of days of which this one, concrete now and in which the light
seems solid as any *ding-an-sich*, comes to the window
in a somewhat placatory, over-familiar
manner as if it were here already and what you saw
wasn't light slipping from the hill — the way it just opens
or blocks out space sometimes — its dumb instrumentality.

The Honeymooneers

The book opens on it:
the yard, the seminary
and collapsing barns,
iron crosses and their

abandon among sunshine and thick grass,
a taste of red or communion wine
— we, too, drunk probably —
the way the bell tower prolonged itself

the shadow of it turning on the grass,
a honeycomb moon. And *here*:
so much green and white of clouds,
plaster, heron's belly — the child

shouting in the shuttered street —
suddenly airy in this winter kitchen
with the sleeping stove, the man
asleep upstairs like Hopkins' benison,

boots by the doorway.
Two *presents*. Neither giving
anything to the other. The mind's eye
shuttering, shuttering each open.

From the Scots

A small plane drifts on the sky.
It's hot. My toes uncurl.
Bees jockey at heather. Robins skirl
in the thicket. I lie

nearly flat on a recliner
watching flies jump and wait
for you: *not yet*. It's late
in summer, early for us:

while borders fall open,
grow grotesque, we turn
over tight as possession,
knit small and bright, mend

nothing. Our garden leans
into the sky. Beyond this
is beauty, grief,
whatever it is we mean,

big words darkening
in a blue receding arc.

Into the Dark

We are so far into the nowhere already — long
shadows of trees stretching and yawning, a fine frost — we
are so far along, you and I and this sleeping pet who
carries curled in him (folded, put away for the winter
but still present, lying in lines, witness to itself) the shape
of that other, the one who went missing, whose story is
an unformed — a *nothing* — we need to feel the size and weight
of, a curled-up sleek memory of the familiar cat
suddenly stepping from the what-is to the maybe, cat-
wise into the dark: or the flush of white bellies those doves
flutter in sunlight — wing shutter — flutter up into the
not-yet — *where*? and how do they know which way to go? —
cat? doves? or how do we move in or because of the —
nowhere — we already live in, breathe in and out of?

Wulf and Eadwacer

from the Anglo-Saxon

It's like a gift to these people.
If he mounts a raid they mean to take him out.
We're separated.
Wulf's on one island, I'm on another:
it's secure, surrounded by bog
and the locals are killers.
If he mounts a raid they mean to take him out.
We're separated.
I've cried for Wulf, longed for him from a distance.
When it was rainy and I was sad
the war hero took me in his arms.
That brought me joy but also pain.
Wulf, Wulf, it's waiting for you
that's making me ill; that you take so long coming
makes me pine away, not being hungry.
Eadwacer, can you hear me? A wolf
will carry our poor child off to the forest.
People can easily break apart what's uncompleted:
the story of us.

How It Was

We clicked our fingers
and suddenly, easily, you were there,
little spark shooting
in the dark between us,
in the cool imagined space of the scan.

You were a star
with a pumpkin head; a nursery rhyme;
you were our accidental shaving
a spiral cast-off from the bench;
you flickered like something to steer by.

That was how it was,
driving over the dark mountains
towards the image of you
I imagined on the windscreen;
the Irish music playing on the seat beside us

sounding as if they knew everything
and we nothing. You were at the heart of it,
making me feel like sick jelly
because I loved you.
That was how it was

in the cold trolley
— what some nurse got for Christmas —
not saying goodbye to you.
But then there was only I
and the flat dream of a friend

coming to the hospital to get me:
and I alive, unshocked
and you safe from love
and all its injuries.
Between the trees' dark spaces, though,
something stayed unbridged.

Logging the Windfall

Dusk comes in
   and closes the window
and downstairs the vivid sound
   of the fireguard
      scrape of a chairleg

suggests what darkness hides
   is tiny, alert movement
like a rat's eye
   or someone listening for you
      your own small scrapes

and turns
   like mistakes, like clues
as to what you're doing,
   though you're doing nothing
      or nearly nothing:

muddling the white page
   making muck stick
like combs of dirt
   on the dog's belly
      like field tracks

showing what happened this afternoon,
   whether it was fun
or you argued, how the dog
   jumped when the dead tree
      gaped and shrank

the light on the sawblade
  you probably imagined
and ivy dust: something small
  but it might
      have been important

might have started or suggested
  a myth or a quarrel
or the gleaming actual
   — how you were laughing
    or him.

Putting the Field Together

And moving between oak leaves the light flurries, thickens, hot
yellow like the wax of a day candle, swirls and drips as
it opens up what is from what may be, thrusting it up
— the is — with the singlemindedness of a yellow flame
— a tongue — a singleminded abruption that is a
gesture neither for us nor including any audience
at all, that is therefore a going on and growing up
not at all like what we've been doing (referential, sly
with our fear of rejection) but instead a kind of
bluntness which arrogates all the fields behind the trees so
that they're turning yellow, the winter wheat sprouts yellow, the
loam is yellow, even the foliage rubs yellowness
out of itself, a sullen fireburst, and chucks up
on us whatever it chucks, violently: and so it goes.

The Separation

After she'd gone, I began to ask
myself and the other ones there too
— some you could see, others were keeping
to the walls — about what she had said.

I could have taken her whole speech a-
part. Or was it me her words broke up?
I felt my knees, feet, elbows leave me,
not in that order though, they just went

and flickered back, and then went again
off like mudslips, sudden and sodden
with me crying. I was howling by
then of course, hiccupped ululations

though I doubt she heard me. Her own words
ringing like sirens, like holy bells
— vindication of a sacred heart —
in the ears she carried off with her.

That was a new kind of martyrdom.
I was falling apart in there. But
as luck would have it you missed all that,
breasts on a plate, the arrows, Romans

betting on our domestic lions.
Grief is a show. But not a big one.
That's what I realised, waking up
once to another morning of it,

a dawn with stretch-marks of grief on its
belly already. I had to get
out of that room, that terrible team
The Incredible Losers. I walked.

I talked the walk. I told those others,
my dumb allies, where I was going.
Few responded. They were afraid. I
remember them now, crowding like ghosts

at the furthest reaches of firelight
that their eyes made something of. I waved,
jaunty, though I felt myself drowning
in darkness — invisible still, remember,

my fingers glued like a toy bear's, lids
dragging gravel over squint pupils,
thighs turned to jelly — it's quite a climb
out of the cave into broad daylight

and when I reached the surface, blinking
and clearing the nocturnal phlegm, I
paused not so much for effect as to
effect a better start in the Land

of Visible Enfranchisement. Drew
powerful breath. Began then to move
slow as a steam motor'd thing at first
then, learning it, with increasing grace,

a gathering sensation of what
was getting to be special about
this whole affair already. I grew
hair and lashes, smell, colour and sound

in that first week, but stuck a while on
touch. That took some patience. Then it came.
And came and came, the cold scream of ice,
the hum of rock, wood pliant as skin

the world bringing me back my shed limbs
— ornery, stiff, but prickly with life —
like the intuition that got me
to her door at last. I thought I saw

how it was, now, in the land of the
living. Thought I knew the ropes. So fell,
like you would have predicted, right off
the map. Since I was her disappeared

my appearance was dis-obit,
was disobedience. Forbidden
fruit. I hung on a while in that fork
not getting it, till she called me back,

told me *Go get stuffed*. I baked alright
in the fire of that. Remembered those
wall-seekers. This was what scared them! I
thought about the tomb I'd waited in,

that place of terminations, stations
without comforts, a clearing house for
filial failure. *I can't go on
I can't go on, I'll go on.* And I

began to walk again, into the
broad view and all that it promises,
green and gilt and full of trees under
none of which I saw my mother sit.

Walking, Flying

Alive? And — yes — yes — long wingbeats knock it out of
                                                    the sky,
silver out of lead, ground darkening but the moon high as
tree tops, black piercing black and white racing through
                                        black — wings
bent heavy as boomerangs with feathers', tendons', bones' rise
and rhythmic give — as if light splayed feathers, dived, crashed
                                                    the white
river or heron rose continual, indefinite,
dragging with it the dark water, hauling through sky something
— what? — dragging with it something not yet formed —
                                        the taste of dusk
going green — out of the formless full valley the white fields
black copses out of memory out of the smell of wood
the path the black dog racing longlegged under hawthorn
the heron bringing up another walk — in rain, thunder —
ten years ago, here — picture it skating up over dark
trees, smooth as a moon — and the bird and I are still living.

The Hand, Dreaming

And then the texture of it. The meet
skin arranges between itself and — *cold* —
the white paint the hand meets
falling again through the room's shutter

falling
like a wing broken at the
wrist, like an eyelid;
white and darkness. The hand's print

moisture on the wall
springing away from the paint's
skin. Momently, the wall under the palm
or the palm's warmth

on the white wall in which the hand understands
— *nothing* —
while the moment
flaps like a loose hand.

What is it?
The waiting, moving hand
which you could have missed,
the handfuls of — *something* —

the palm tensing for resistance,
the fluttering pulse,
the meet flexing and going.

Landscapes After Verlaine

from Poèmes Saturniens

I

Shepherd's Delight

The moon's red on the cloudy horizon;
Smokily, in a shimmying fog,
The plain dozes; and a frog calls
From green reeds a shiver runs through;

Water lilies close their crowns up again;
Poplars in proper lines
Profile a faraway vague ghostliness;
Fireflies waver among the bushes;

Tawny owls wake and noiselessly
Row the black air with their heavy wings
And the high sky fills with dim stars.
In a shock of white, Venus emerges: and it's night.

II
Autumn Number

In autumn
the drawn-out sobs
   of violins
infect me
with dreary
   listlessness.

Suffocating,
pale, whenever
   the clock strikes
I remember
the old days and
   break down;

and I'm off
on a rough wind
   which carries me
here and there
like
   a dead leaf.

III
Deep Water

The loud ocean
Beats under the eye
Of the grieving moon
And beats again

While a brutal
Threatening light
Splits the darkened night
With a long bright zigzag

And while, in convulsive leaps
Along the reefs
Each wave comes, goes,
Shining and tight:

And when the whole sky
Where a hurricane's loose
Shakes terrifyingly
With thunder.

Cut Glass

It seemed that in the new vividness (the air like water
tearing brightly the iris refracting) you could go out
(feeling the cold splash and break as you moved through it)
                                                                         to the
rose bushes and search doggedly, with an intelligence
urgent yet local, your fingers getting the hang of it
again (the light on your neck a shock like the time you jumped
in the lake from the borrowed boat), for and clip out these small
furled but perhaps sentient heads which smell so little of
something forgotten and which in the glass seem to fall a-
part already but still, still, like the pale thread *you* hang on
are themselves, a complex plenty with checks and balances,
not stuttered, unexchanged, their pink-yellow petals old and
veined already, their invisible perpetual
motion starring the rooms you swim through stroke after
                                                                      stroke —

Hotel Boulevard

Waking up in this spaciousness — the air
    is absolutely dry, is empty
of anything like sweat or moisture, you
    could dry bathe in it surely —
as if suddenly arrived on the perfect
    dryness of a legendary island shore
— as if beyond "arrived" in fact, as if
    cast up by the smooth wave
of having-been-already: the water and
    time moving smoothly on each other
as silk — you are first of all glad.
    Glad that the stainless day
in which you have arrived without illness
    is already there below your window,
the black widow and vans and the
    yellow Dacia taxis,
glad that your body is brown and dry
    and smooth with the heat
and of course you are glad of the
    terraces verandas lindens
and the Moorish arcades of the embassy district
    in between all of which the heat
already moves without demands like an underfed cat.
    And then you know
that your companion's awake in this
    perfect heat and that he
too arrived like a beached boat over the tideline:
    completely. So that your own completeness
shifts a little. Now there are two
    completenesses. And if two, why not

two million and two? The city suddenly filling up
    around you with clamour and dust,
the scaffolding and the satellite dishes and
    three stray dogs across the road right now
all justified by this electric light
    and by the case of completeness
whose alterity you respect as much
    as a stranger's footprint as you
turn to him, wanting to take away and
    to take this strangeness.

Hors d'Oeuvre

Blunt-nosed omnivores, we
sit at the door
and toy with bananas *à la Greque* or, worse,
a mug of Pau D'Arco tea

freshly picked-up from the deli,
the supermarket.
And we're not alone.
The swifts, too, are snacking

— though perhaps with a sharper
diction — on gnats,
bees, the plankton of the air
which is also like wine of course

this summer evening
— also blue, like toasted
lobster, split blackberry-and-
apple soufflé, blueberry muffin

or crêpe, the checked blue of our napkin.

Tracking

All along the track the alder trunks are liminal, are
tracking, almost, the progress of pallor, are falling in
to or behind the condition of morning (a state of
light — its movement or weight —) as if they were lined-up,
beyond the pale of noon and the eventual farmhouse,
to turn away history; as if the whole matter of
morningness were purely private, like moving into an
embrace; as if it were local, taking place — *morning* —
without movement but lightly: the whitey-pink pales and
sideways light tipping the tilled-up soil (its exact grade and
loaminess) and the screech-cock; as if morning only came
to this especial field (and with difficult — *delicacy*)
clinging to white palings which are young alders and
tracing the white dirt to which they tend, where they lead
                                                                            the eye.

Getting the Results

Odd to get it all back — this —
with colour and so on, I mean

with that sense — like prayer — slipping
away or out or under of some duty

some dutiful attention or care with which
one might handle the whole of — this —

brought up short like that
by its possible absence, a shift in which

what you relied on was — nothing —
this — was nothing

in which the stove the kettle the airer
and the cat at the firebox door: slippage

you couldn't take up or for granted:
a flash — glitter — now that you're

well, perhaps impossible.

The X File

It doesn't matter what I say or do,
You don't love me. That's the end of it.
Doesn't matter that I loved so well
I lost myself in keeping sight of you.
No gifts, no words, no tendernesses prove
Truths that you untell, the proofs you fell
Blind to logic, making stories fit
The way your shoulder used to, or the tender groove
Between your thumb and palm that once clipped mine
Neat as a file, holding knowledge tight:
That you were mine. You're not tonight.
Instead I travel on, through dark so fine
You might think that was what got in my eyes:
And not the strain of saying these goodbyes.

The Misunderstanding

Those lilies. The space they took.
Now I understand how they flared into life
each lifted lip creamy and abundant
each trumpet a blare of money. Vulgar with optimism

I picked them from their bucket
in a shop where two men were teaching
a labrador tricks. The shady interior
prickled with cellophane.

On the shelf, on your shelf, the birthday lilies
magnetised the light from the lamps
in an autocracy of the sexy.
They seemed a pivot, a vacuum

of all that might happen next
or had. For you they were already
hardening, an image of light and of white
like new walls, a place that might turn out

to be sudden and generous as an Israeli flower
out of the badlands of history
out of dark interiors, a bolt of beauty
with nothing but salvation in mind.

I'd no idea. I sat watching the flowers
drink the light. They were packed with it.
They were a lightshow lasering over
and over extravagant blank cursives.

Drawing the Line

The living line keeping the grass — grass — or the sky
full: where it rises from the paper as if it was there
already like a ghost or miracle waiting to be
moved (and *we're* moved): its unallowed width invisible but
black — a pigment sprinkle at the edge crowding to what
we think of (if we do) as a *whole* — a hole? — running
over, running across the picture like a cut, a
deep otherness making up the picture as if to point
out some kind of fear or resolution holding it in:
light or the raised arm, the ball breaking it
open, breaking it onto the page: the weight of shadow,
the falling line, the way the muscles and tendons must bunch
to it, the loss of whatever it was the moment just
before it was — this — nowness and thisness: this line.

A Family Affair

I
Born 1899: A Costive Incubation

Poor doll. Your tiny hands, your feet
are porcelain. Your feathered hats
nod, sway and incubate
the still air. You know it.

— And I want to pick you up, pick you
up to play with.
I'm six years old. You
teach me that to live

all I need's a white
impervious skin; the tint
applied on lips and cheeks light
enough to hint

there's life within
or not.

II

Born 1932: The Eggshell Cadenza

There's life within. Not
that we approach, broach
the tight shell hot —
sealed, let loose

what nests there. But — pricey,
rare — she
trembles with beauty
like the sideboard glass, the piano-keys

that speak privately
in the close room
of the family:
a space so designated that the new

can't live in or out
of it.

III
Born 1963: Flying the Nest

In and out
the stems, spaliers of the house
I go — quiet
as a stretched twig, alert as a leaf's

end nosing this net
of wood and plaster
that's growing faster than my yet-
unnested future....

In that copse
the unseen trees shake with fruitless
appeal
      — their forecast tops
a synthesis of breath

with limb
that cracks egg to flight.

The Bargain

How the sound moves in the ear, a curve into presence, and
clots as you recognise it — your name, the sound of a car —
as you make it your own or *it is made*: like home-coming
time after time into the ah! of recognition,
into the gaze which will *name* you at last: the sound like a
place to live and move around in, a shelter before the
next — coming — which slides towards you and the focus
you are or make somehow (a resister interrupting
the passage of this or that overtone); you grope for it
and it becomes a handle you can grope along so that
by stairs of sound — upward — a spiral — you climb
from the ear's curve — warm — stretching towards the *other*
which floats without focus — a cat's hair falling — and
is not yet — can't — will be as you move into it.

Draft for a Short Fiction

When they brought me to see him the first time it must have been
summer but I don't remember that.
The day outside the windows was a faraway and hung up
flag (probably faded) and the windows were big white frames.
He was in the second of a row of chairs I think.
They were sort of a peachy plastic. He was in the second from left
as you came in. We came in.
He was crossing his legs. His jaw chewed (but not his
mouth), it was a slow
stretching. At times I used to think (after
the guard had gone, after we were alone
together in the locked day room)
that his whole skeleton (he was very thin)
could stretch like this, it was as if he stretched towards you
as if he was all tentacles
and his eyes stretched back wide in his head.
He was like a space man. You couldn't be sure
whether he understood this. He said *I am an alien*.
He was untenable. The sun came and filled the windows
and he was the alien, the fisheyed god. You could see light
                                              through his fingers.
There was a panic button by the door. He was twenty-two.
He was the world.
The illness chewed and translated him. He had trainers and jeans.
He smelt of gum and lilies. There were things he knew. When he
got clever the illness waited for him. His chair was always the
                                                same one.
He head turned into a cube, he was a receptor. The illness looked
blandly out of his eyes at me.
His voice as was stac-stac-static. Sometimes
the guard forgot our tea.

Fear of Drowning

The ferns are pressing on the glass.
They're pale. They tremble and turn grey.
I'm waiting for my dream to pass.

The room shakes off the drifting dark
As if it celebrated day,
The ferns are pressing on the glass

Like hands preparing for the task
Of closing on themselves to pray,
I'm waiting for my dream to pass

With all those meanings that I grasp
Distinctly, though I turn away.
The ferns are pressing on the glass.

They fray, they breathe, suggest the task
Of cutting down, clearing away.
I'm waiting for my dream to pass.

Each morning I wake to this loss,
To daylight setting terms to pay.
The ferns are pressing on the glass.
I'm waiting for my dream to pass.

Folding the Real

> *Violinists believe older instruments, in particular, retain*
> *the 'voice' of their owner even when borrowed or sold.*
> *The result is a kind of ventriloquy.*

The *voice* — that print of self — which is already in
the unmade sound, which is in the ear or comes up to meet
the sound you make, the belly another voicebox to mirror
your own (intimate with the kind of knowledge you didn't
mean to let slip) the hair a tain dividing, uniting
the sound you will make and the one already made, the sound
waiting with the one actualising — being —
in the spacious way of waves (moving out to something more,
endlessly spreading and branching in a tree of pitches,
knocking out the ends of the possible a little), while
the given is a folding over into itself, a
repetition, registering the possible and what's
beyond it and drawing up to the surface, up through the
wood and wire and stain, the print of self: that is, of what is.

Dear Emma

The child comes
out of the half-
real realm, out
of the cloudiness

with which we talked,
you and I (lying
on our backs
in the dark in

the bedroom)
when we used
to wonder what
our babies would be

like. The child
comes with arms
out like a doll's
perspicuous and foreign

like an agent. Which
she is, in a
way. Her citizen-
ship of the

mysterious world is
plain like an accent.
(She does everything
a new way. She's

packed with
secrecy. She conducts
long private congress
with herself.) Who

can imagine what
she knows? Only
she bears
her three strange gifts.

*Desire, touch,
calculation*: who
can bear the strange
script drifting

by when she
unseals her bright
pertinent eyes?

—The world
of the sky, my
dear: she and
you. You and I.

What Furniture Does

Space fills and empties. Space filling and emptying. This is
how objects get away. Once in possession they begin
that weird flexing of light, air and so on, they take up the
question of volume quite seriously and noisily
even, in fact you wish they would stop sometimes:
                                            there are, you
say, enough scientists already doing this sort of
thing and what you want to do is stop the shouting, make love
and peace and just get wise to everything: except you know
how it will turn out, the objects getting to impinge on
each other so that neither you nor he will be able
to sort out what started where but hear, in the quiet that
follows each engagement — in which each blade of grass,
                                                   each plate
as it were indulges in an obfuscatory post-
coital smoke — the long rumble of retreating power: of things.

Pastoral from a Millennial Pattern-Book

The nuns' cows are coming, all porcelain
ornament and exquisite movement,
down the East Hayfield;

a hatch clatters in the notched oak;
birds slip with soft
tearing sounds through superheated air.

Sea-shadows below this field are like stains:
signs, not meant,
of deepening reality

where we float
among the white tossed
clover, cultivate our cares.

— And after the Millennium, what remains?
Or what's here now? For this scene's only lent
— it's got an eighteenth-century feel —

from a pattern-book;
and every pastoral returns to loss,
cow-like, with conscientious care.

Wye

riddle for a stonework

I am a question that never ends
I am green water, ox-bow bends

I am gravity's perpetual motion
And I am a map of the way to the ocean.

I am the sap in the slap of the cricket bat
I am the mason of boundary and flat

I'm cuckoo and cricket and ferret's cry
Don't ask *what* I am but *Wye*.

Travel Diary

The sill is also a horizon. You lie down below it
on the blanket bed
     to watch trees and grass screen
the pale shiftiness

which is a continent of distance. Timber yards fill
                                          the screen
with pale ash-bark
     thin part-spectrum light
a page's pallor

and you mark the page. *Szajol*. But it could be
have been
     somewhere else, the bony trees all illusion
the glassy leaves

full of a pale river's light numinous
the way an accent
     catches a word
— palely loitering — on the edge

moving past perception. The anxious
Serb. Black flax
     on reeds beyond glass.
A pale litter of stubble.

All this already paling and cooling to memory.
You read it again.
     You'll read it again.
Two children in an apple tree

still balancing there. Light is in the sky's
white screen
     on the page
on your foreigner's tongue.

Metamorphosis

Your fingernails grew like roaches all week and you could not
do anything about the way her father terrified
her still, the way he was and wasn't there and how he seemed
to his daughter at age eight or nine like a storm cloud in
the centre of which was electricity but which was
never still enough for her to find or hold to the far
side of the hill from that centre so she keeps a distance
still behind enormous pebble lenses which make her seem
stupid although her blond bob's immaculate and her shirt
respectably African and when she laughs it's loud, deep
like the coffee colour her eyes brew up for the morning
after, the days after that childhood she recovered or
recovers from like your own fear loathing and love of your
child self which had scuttled like a roach in and out all week.

Viznar by Moonlight: Two poems after Lorca

I
The Moon's Up

When the moon rises
bell towers fall silent
and overgrown paths
clear.

    When the moon rises
the sea covers the land
and love feels like it's an island
in the infinite.

    Nobody eats oranges
in the flood of moonlight.
You have to eat
frozen green fruit.

    When the moon rises
on a hundred similar faces
the silver pieces
sob in their purse.

II
The Night of Loving Sleeplessly

Night above the two of us. With a full moon.
I began to cry for myself and you laughed.
Your disdain was a god, my sobbing
moments and chained doves.

Night below the two of us. A crystal of grief,
you wept through profound distances.
My pain spent itself
on the sand of your weak heart.

Dawn had us on the bed together,
mouths on the freezing jet
of blood endlessly spending itself:

and the sun came through the balcony enclosure
and the coral of life opened and branched
over my already half-buried heart.

Sestina for an Ice Age

If it's what you want I'll do it: pull
the shutters down, go underground, freeze,
dry up like the red runnels in quartz....
You see I've always known
you're the pearl of great price, not
to be buried or scratched at any price, rare

in the way my gloss is rare:
changing the affair, yet feeling the pull
west of my heart's balance — not
like a weathercock's or barometer freeze
but down an unwritten line, unparsable but known
by the intuition that guides miners to quartz

seams and sequins in old quartz-
caulked quarries; that, buried like mineral, on rare
moments flickers, nevertheless, morse: the known
tragedy, that strange pull
away from the doomed plane, the way you freeze
when love walks in the room. Not

that following my heart's easy. It's not.
The needle's still shaky, tremulous as quartz
held up to the light, and the long freeze
isn't done yet. In the Black Hills the light's rare,
Spring only a light greening on slopes where scree pulls
at new roots. What's known

is only as carrion's known.
Lambs, families die of painful exposure, not
through fault, but because the dark pulls
so hard at our feet on these quartz
slopes. So the living heart's rare
bud must survive this freeze:

yet you want to freeze
it. And yet, if I had known
this price, your rare
heart-tax, I would not
have hesitated. ...Quartz
clicks the minute hand along like snow. You pull

me on, into the rare freeze.
Where we're going's not yet known.
Your lodestone pull's like quartz.

The Pull of Air

Of course it all depends on effort, on that leavening
which makes it spring into being, in other words when he
takes the heavy hammer, already feeling the effort
— through arm, shoulder, chest, hip and right down to his
                                                  knees in the
too-big spare jeans — as a kind of load, a payment the pull
of air exacts from the (imagined) fin he might steer with
if the not-yet space he's making could be steered in or through;
or else like a counter-balance to the returning spring
of effort from his feet up (braced calves) marking out its
own potential as it comes (his fingers white with brick dust):
a warm rising note of metal on brick and breeze block which
fills the house and garden you've so casually taken
on, so everything has that stink of promise you fell for
yourselves: air fluently carving, meanwhile, its way
                                                  through walls.

Icarus in a Rainstorm (Six Views)

Seeing
how the fluid line of the horizon
expanded
          a string vibrating
to the high note of flight
                    he flew

feeling the silk of rain
on his arms
the satin air around him

          *

between the window rail
and the car park
he flickered like the inside
of an eyelid
a glimpse of height
an almond descending curve
something lighter than
                  rain
falling
into the sodium glare

          *

hair feathering his nape

          *

rain-made rips and stars in the
hospital evening
his hands starry
full of darkness
the lights

      flying

he threw out meaning
a living line *around the earth in forty minutes*
and the horizon waxed
and waned

      *

the way a gull struggles
in high wind
advances
    — flexes
        — moves across the view
he flew

seemed almost to float a moment
filling the window.

Legal and Tender

When the telephone rings unexpectedly or my neighbour
ties her dogs to the gatepost and comes in
to talk about the buyer she just got
or I'm in the bath and add things up:

what comes to mind's
people with lives that are legal and tender,
that they can keep warm in their hands. Petals
on the porch floor, colour photographs

with everyone in frame, food
only an afterthought and (we're British) really
not that much to get excited over.
And in the park their kids kicking a ball

each foot landing right, while overhead
the punctual planes come safely in, rain falls
in punctuating well-anticipated showers and everything
is natural without end right to the end.

The Science of Memory

"The flats forget their places. They swell up
on either side of roads that used to go
to town and back. Their brittle windows glow
at teatime, till each modest curtain shuts

the fading district — barricaded, gapped
like boxers' mouths with gold and shadows — out.
Beyond this block the street falls prey to doubt.
What happened to those shops where awnings flapped

all day like something struggling to get free?
And where's the bus stop, that would set down right
at Maypole's, weekdays hourly, tabled tight
as children's stories, home in time for tea?

The clouds are lifting. Someone shouts. Then laughs.
A bike revs up. Two kids come out to play.
So my old bones will last another day
I think, and cross the street onto the grass

that lines the pavement just beyond the lights.
I know it all. Each inch is mine. I see
my life's been fixed by struggles to get free
of what dissolves in gentleness and night."

The Fattening

A morning like this when anything smells fresh and anything will
do, the bicycle gleaming with rain against the coal store
under the bathroom window and smudged grey clouds coming in
as if there were no difference between rain and the threat
of rain while everything keeps on moving and shining like
it does now: the hens busy with their mud and the stupid
tender-eyed terrier racing for the late wasp which stops
just for now on your finger then shakes itself — like the ear
of your sentimental dog, a drip fattened on the clothes-
line gathering itself for flight, the rust blooming no doubt
under the bicycle saddle or in the brackets of
your bench — splits, dives and just misses the dog's snap though
                                                                      its brown
plush darkens with wet like a child's stained dress, a blush, or the
reservations you want the light to make bright, fantastic.

Green Thought

Stealthy as any unicorn he
drops his capsule among the books:
knowing that unreason, like ink, runs
the more you rub at it.

Inexpungeable, alert, with muddied fingers
poised like a chef's, he
sows the brilliant flowers
that hedge the child's dreams

and pout in the dreams
of her parents. The readers sleep.
Poetry jumps ship from her shelf
and stalks into the moonlight:

she's the songster and the bloodied
shroud. Our heroine
clenches her hand to the bedhead again:
sweet Jack, nimble Jack's come calling.

I

The bird rises to my surprise:
small and exact like Kate's hands
it bursts the wood's cover
and disappears on some urgent chartered errand.

Such will is Kate's too;
they're two white knights
building watchtowers, looking around
for a view. Their frankness appals

like morning air let in
too soon. Underfoot, though,
the earth turns — darker than you'd expect.
It hugs its density to itself:
irreconcilable.

II

The last thing you
see isn't white
or blue. It's

pubic fuzz, the soft scrim
of trees going
left off the picture.

That's what I dream about.
The old country going down
the drain, the whole

Channel a plug
in some big picture.
And last of all

that tree-tangle
coming over clear
while the

hills, (glimpsed only
intermittently)
go down, as your

boat strains
among the big waves
and you search

with mounting
desperation for
the sandbank.

III

Half-folded, half-finished, the new leaves
spring at our step. They're pale
as the small hairs running
over your ears. Surprisingly,

they ripple; and the ripple runs
on and on to our left.
Perhaps it comes back in the dark
having gone left for ever?

I like to lie in the wood's cover
like a Welshman, dreaming
how that sudden autonomous vigour
transfigures our too-ready clinch.

IV

Marsh-mallow, beeswax, marjoram,
white-nettle. The old straight tracks are
too blunt for this landscape. *Catnip.*
Cuckoospit. In the back seat
the child retches and retches
with desire to step out
into the white fields of willowherb.

The sun tracks the endless
rural sky. *Nightshade, nectarine, lady's finger.*
The petals fall from the daisy. Walls
run over the view like tracking stitches;
Ellsburys tack to Stonestreets, Hancocks
to Frys. She dreams
(as the little pile of petals grows)

of slow waltzes among the
thigh-brushing hay. Cows star
the horizon. She feels herself fall.
The dikes are bubbling their rich uneven potion:
golden seal, comfrey, thyme
the great healer.

*You'll know where I am, although
I shan't pull branches down on you or
send streams leaping in your path. No! Rather
I'll linger on high banks where*

*the light is changeable; I'll shadow you,
Spring lovers, on your roundabout tramps, mock
your stoutheartedness (knowing
the delicacy with which you come to flower*

*in the Hostel baths)... I'll be your tain,
I'll thicken up the day for you with my quick
silver. How does your heart beat?
Steady as your feet? I'll make it skip.*

*I'll plant secrets in every tree
and you — listen, babes — you'll walk
a hundred irradiated fields
on my verklärte trail.*

By Your Self

None of it matters of course, none of it matters now, you
might say as you wait for the scan or stare at that other
(tedious, familiar) who accompanies you on
this journey as on so many others: this journey: there,
you're saying it already like there's far to go but you
may be fine, *fine* and all of this a rehearsal, a short
walk in another place you don't live, it may be nothing
but your fear (your fear and your doctor's) the scan may
                                                                            not show
any fat white patches, doodles on your soft precious lights
and liver, you may be going to live for ever or
if not for ever for now which is the same thing, it's *life*
it's now, stretching out again, it's a place in the rigging
it's your own story and not the one in the mirror it's

Acknowledgements

Acknowledgements are due to the editors of the following publications where some of these poems first appeared: *Agenda, Alternatives: Social Transformation and Humane Governance, London Magazine, Metre, North Dakota Quarterly,* (in Romanian translation) *Observator Cultural* (Bucharest), *Over Milkwood* (Alun Books, 2000), *Oxygen* (Seren, 2000), *Poetry Wales, Slope, The Healing Arts* (OUP, 1994), *The Interpreter's House, Thumbscrew, Verse.*

'Dear Emma' is taken from *BirthChart* (1992), a sequence of poems with printmaker Meg Campbell, commissioned by Southern Arts with Southampton City Gallery, which also formed part of the Usher Gallery, Lincoln's touring exhibition *Reclaiming the Madonna* (1993). 'A Family Affair' was commissioned by Southern Arts for *My Grandmother, My Mother, Myself* (1995), a touring exhibition of artists' books and poetry, now in the permanent collection of Johannesburg City Gallery. 'Wye' was commissioned by Wycombe District Council (1997) for works with stone-carver Alec Peever (1995). 'The Science of Memory' formed part of Age Concern England's Debate of the Age in Swindon (1998) and of Ledbury Poetry Festival's Shell House programme (1999).

'Green Thought' won the 1992 Oxford University Newdigate Prize.

'Folding the Real' and 'The Bargain' are taken from *Sprung Release*, a radio piece written with Pauline Stainer and commissioned by Southern Arts. Some of these poems were broadcast on *Nightwaves* (BBC R3), Radio Wales, BBC Radio Oxford, BBC Wiltshire Sound and Romanian National Radio (English Language Service). 'Dear Emma' forms the basis of a *lieder*-cycle by Christopher Bochmann (Lisbon, 1994)

Acknowledgements are due to the Oppenheimer-John Downes Memorial Awards, to the Arts Council of Wales for a Writer's Award, to the Society of Authors for an award, to the Millay Foundation, New York for a Residency and to Southern Arts for a Writer's Award which enabled work on this collection.

I'd particularly like to thank Tim Liardet for his resourceful patience with this book and its author.